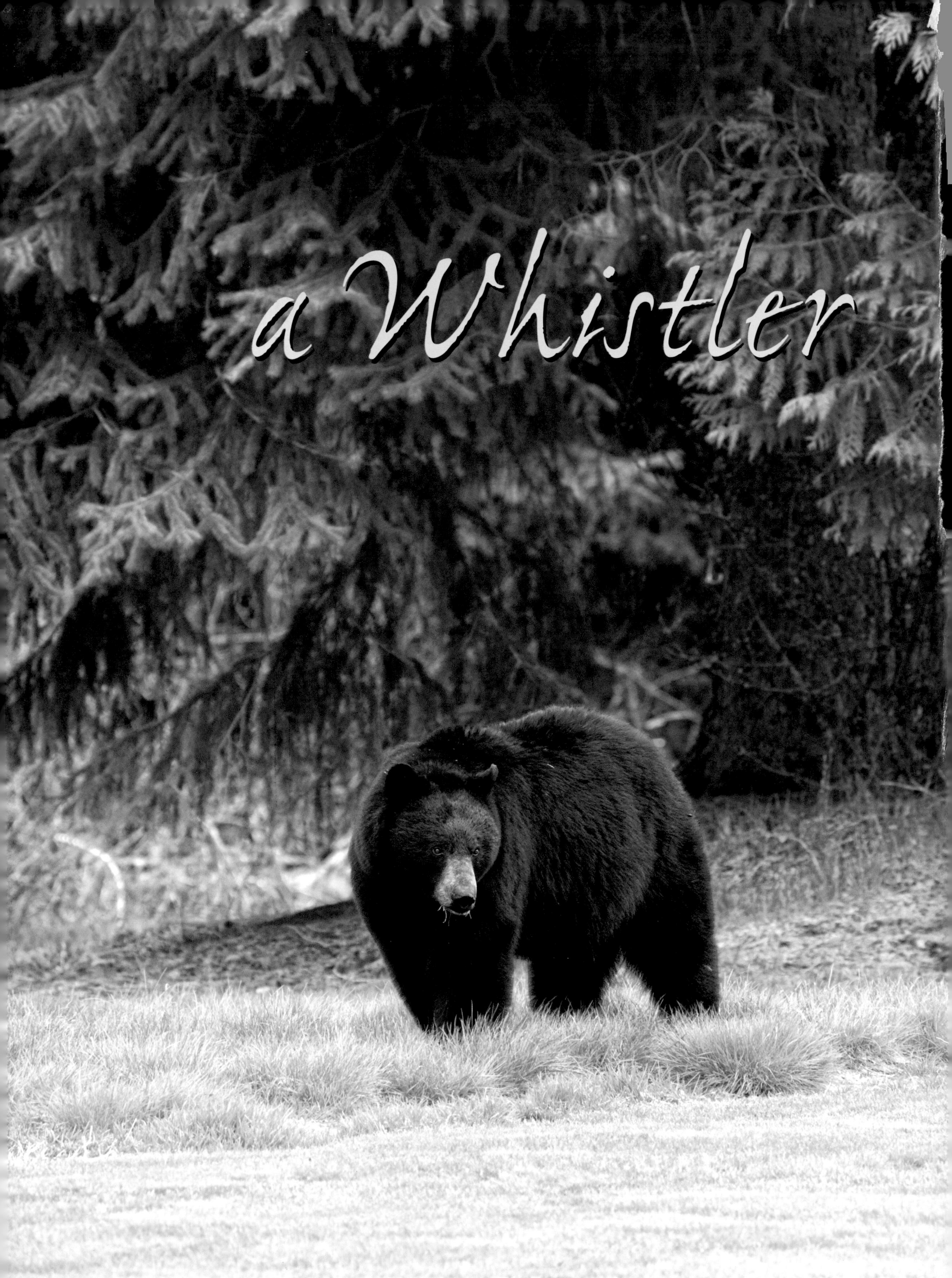
a Whistler

BEAR STORY

SYLVIA DOLSON
& KATHERINE FAWCETT

Sincere thanks to David Krughoff for his hard work and expertise,
and to Lori Homstol, John Stoddart, David Burke and Clare Ogilvie for their wise input.
We are also grateful to the Vancouver Foundation
for their generous financial support.

Written by Sylvia Dolson and Katherine Fawcett
Photography by Sylvia Dolson
Book Design by Fiona Raven

First Printing January 2010
Printed and bound in Canada by Friesens

Published by
Get Bear Smart Society
P.O. Box 502
Whistler, BC V0N 1B0
www.bearsmart.com

Library and Archives Canada Cataloging in Publication

Dolson, Sylvia
A Whistler bear story / Sylvia Dolson and Katherine Fawcett.

ISBN 978-0-9813813-0-5

1. Black bear–British Columbia–Whistler Region. 2. Black bear–behaviour–British Columbia–Whistler Region. 3. Black bear–Effect of habitat modification on–British Columbia–Whistler Region. 4. Black bear–Effect of human beings on–British Columbia–Whistler Region. I. Fawcett, Katherine, 1967– II. Get Bear Smart Society III. Title.

QL737.C27D64 2009 599.78'5 C2009-906474-X

For Slip and Fitz
and all the bears that have lost their lives
as a result of conflict with people.

Bear Stories

You hear them everywhere. In the gondola. At the pub. Around the campfire.

Some are endearing tales—two chubby cubs wrestle and somersault together on the grassy slope under the Wizard chairlift on a sparkling spring morning. Some are frightening—a 300-pound male bluff-charges a mountain biker on a trail near Lost Lake. Some are tragic—an 18-year-old mother bear is killed after she develops a taste for the easy calories in garbage and wanders through the back door of a café. And some are just plain weird—a young mother bear breaks into a Whistler condo and gently but thoroughly licks the homeowner's cat.

Black bears are as much a part of Whistler as alpine lakes, fresh snow and clear mountain air. They were here before the first slope was skied, before the first golf ball was teed. They wandered the neighbourhoods of Alpine, Emerald and Bayshores long before any ski cabins or resort homes were built. And they ambled down Highway 99 when it was a trail of huckleberry bushes and creeks. As city dwellers discovered the joys of this mountain playground, bears discovered the joys of human food, and a fragile coexistence began.

Today, Whistler has approximately 10,000 permanent residents, 11,500 second homeowners, 2,500 seasonal workers, two million annual visitors, and an estimated 100 black bears.

While it's true that much of our development—homes, roads, businesses and parking lots—has reduced their habitat, black bears actually thrive in some manmade spaces. Ski hills, golf courses, parks and power-line cuts offer improved feeding for bears. In fact, bears are able to find more of the clover, berries, dandelions and fresh grass they love in a tree-lined meadow or at the edge of a ski run than they can in the dense forest.

Whistlerites have a unique relationship with these ursine beauties. We feel blessed to live in an area where bears inhabit the wilderness. We understand their power. They are tolerant of us, and we are protective of them. We know many of them by name. We follow their antics in the local newspapers and in some cases we know their life stories. And we love casually telling our bear tales to city friends.

However, the human-bear relationship is a fragile one. It can only exist if humans don't feel their safety is at risk. Human fear, whether justified or not, can lead to an unfortunate ending for the bear, who may be killed to ease our collective fears.

Only by preventing bears from losing their natural wariness of humans, making changes to how we deal with bear attractants and replacing old fears with understanding and respect can we reduce conflicts between bears and people. Whistler is proving that it is possible to coexist with bears.

Reverence and Respect

Bears' enormous, luxurious bodies, soulful eyes and quiet but potentially fierce nature have inspired awe, dread and curiosity across cultures and throughout history. They have been both worshipped as earthly incarnations of ancestors or gods and sacrificed for medicinal and ritualistic purposes. It is difficult to think of another mammal that has inspired such a tapestry of mythologies, legends, ceremonies and festivals to honour and appease them.

Archaeological evidence from 50,000 years ago suggests that bear worship, also known as the Bear Cult or Arctolary, may have been practiced by Neanderthals in the Palaeolithic period. The Ainu people of northern Japan considered the bear to be the head of the gods. Celts worshipped bears as earthly incarnations of the goddess Artio. Evidence of bear ceremonies and bear worship has been found among Finns and Lapps of northern Europe. First Nations cultures throughout North America honour the bear with costumes, masks and images carved on totems.

Ursa Major, Latin for Great Bear, is one of the most prominent constellations in the night sky. Although the star pattern has been interpreted differently around the world, it is interesting to note that a number of separate cultures assigned the image of the bear to the star group that crosses the sky each night.

The common, cross-cultural theme in bear mythology is reverence for the bear.

From Killers to Clowns

European traders and settlers arrived on North American shores with weapons—guns, traps and deadly poisons—never seen before, putting bears at man's mercy. As pioneers cleared land for their homes and explorers mapped out new territories, bears were slaughtered. Grizzlies were virtually exterminated from the Canadian Plains and the western United States. In some areas, bounties encouraged hunters to kill as many bears as possible. Stories from hunters, settlers and explorers often portrayed the bear as a man-eating monster.

By the 20th century, public attitudes toward bears began to shift. The creation of national parks coincided with the growing recognition that wildlife deserved a safe place. Laws limiting hunting were enacted, and people began to develop more endearing attitudes toward bears.

Whistler's beloved pioneer Myrtle Philip, hostess of Rainbow Lodge and community icon, kept an orphaned bear cub as a pet, nursing him and hand-feeding him after his mother was killed. Visitors to the lodge loved "Teddy," whose rolly-poly antics provided daily theatre. Philip thought that while it wasn't wise to keep a bear, he would never survive in the wild. She eventually found a home for Teddy at the Vancouver Zoo.

This was an era when the general public tended to view bears as a form of entertainment. Dolled up in tutus, circus bears performed tricks to sold-out crowds. With the advent of the automobile, people began to feel a boldness around bears that they hadn't felt before. Feeding bears was all the rage, and photos of cubs standing up against station-wagon windows abound. In the 1940s and '50s, bear-viewing at garbage dumps became a popular pastime. Bleachers were installed near the Yellowstone Park dump to allow visitors to more comfortably watch the bears feast on campers' leftovers. A large sign on Banff Avenue directed tourists "to the bears" at the town dump. Headlines in the *Edmonton Journal* newspaper promoted Jasper as a fun place to feed bears. Although it was never officially sanctioned in Whistler, bear-viewing at the old, centrally located dump became as common as bird-watching. As many as two-dozen bears could be seen at a time at the Whistler dump, and both visitors and locals knew they could get a show.

Beware of Sensationalism

In books, magazines and movies, bears are media darlings. Audiences are fascinated by bears, whether they are given human characteristics in cartoons, portrayed as merciless killers in movies, or used for advertising. We grew up with the image of the cute 'n' cuddly Disney bear. Winnie the Pooh. Yogi and Boo-Boo . . . they're just goofy, loveable oafs! Remember Gary Larson's cartoon bears? What could be the harm in getting a little closer to the real version for a photo?

The flip side is the image of a terrifying, blood-thirsty stalker like the bear in the 1997 movie *The Edge*. This bear represents the Jaws of the woods, a furry menace who deserves to be destroyed because of his wicked potential. The bear has also been used as a symbol of wisdom, as in the U.S. Forest Service's Smokey Bear, and as a product-hawker such as A&W's Great Root Bear or Coca-Cola's thirsty polar bears. And then there's Grizzly Adams' companion Ben, one of many examples of so-called tame bears living peacefully with humans.

These caricatures do the real bear no favours. False notions and limited understanding can lead to human behaviours that are the cause of most conflicts. As Dave Smith says in his book *Backcountry Bear Basics*, "People can live with real bears. It's the bears roaming the wilds of the human imagination that are impossible to get along with."

That human tragedies have occurred is undisputed. Although rare, each case is indeed horrifying and sad. Statistics may help put these deaths into perspective. According to bear expert Dr. Lynn Rogers, each year in the U.S. and Canada, one in 16,000 people commit murder, whereas one in 35,000 grizzly bears and one in 100,000 black bears kills a human. On average, one person is killed by a black bear every year in North America.

No one has ever been killed by a bear in Whistler. In fact, the chances of being killed by a domestic dog, bees or lightning are much greater than being killed by a bear. However, in British Columbia alone, an average of 824 black bears and 48 grizzlies are destroyed annually by conservation officers because they are considered nuisances or threats to human safety. Hunters shoot another 4,000 bears legally, and an unknown number are killed by poachers and vehicle accidents.

Understanding Black Bears

There is a definite gap between the real and perceived threat of black bears, and typically it's the bears who get the short end of a rather deadly stick. The Get Bear Smart Society is a Whistler-based non-profit organization dedicated to the peaceful coexistence of bears and people. They believe that conflicts can be prevented when people understand bear behaviour and eliminate attractants that draw bears into residential areas.

One common misconception about bears is that they are naturally aggressive. In fact, black bears are inherently timid. When startled, they usually run away—often up a tree in an act of submission. Black bears may appear threatening when standing on their hind legs, but in fact this is how curious bears get a better sense of their surroundings, using smell, sight and hearing. And when bears look like they have their hackles up, it is often just the wind blowing into the fur, making the longer guard hairs rise above the rest of the fur. Even bluff charges are merely meant to communicate that the bear is nervous about your presence and needs more space. There is no doubt that to be bluff charged is an underwear-changing event, but it rarely ends in an attack.

Because of their size and caloric requirements, and because they survive on a mostly plant-based diet, bears are obsessed with food. When they aren't sleeping, bears are generally eating or searching for food. According to local researchers, the average black bear spends 15 to 16 hours per day eating. In the fall prior to denning, a bear may devour up to 50,000 berries and gain three to six pounds in one day.

Like other compulsive eaters, bears have no pride when it comes to what they consume. They aren't terribly picky eaters; if it's available and smells edible, it's fair game to a bear. Human food, including the packaging it was wrapped in, is particularly tantalizing to bears. Leftovers from a dumpster behind a restaurant or dog food on the porch are far easier to find and pack more calories per mouthful than berries, clover or dandelions. In fact, while a pound of huckleberries has a mere 210 calories, a pound of bacon, a favourite breakfast item for many campers, provides approximately 2,500 calories, and a bag of chocolate chip cookies can offer 3,200 calories. The average bird feeder spills out 5,000 to 10,000 calories in one tipping. One of the biggest caloric scores is a 25-pound bag of dry dog food—something many people keep in garages or sheds—with a whopping 42,425 calories!

It doesn't take much to attract a bear. And while he's in the neighbourhood, he might check out what was grilled on the barbecue last night. In the bear's mind, it's a buffet just for him. "Look at that tree laden with ripe apples! A bag of juicy garbage in the shed! And some leftover fast food right through the window of that parked car! Oh, is that a compost pile? Stew for supper! Mmmm . . . a feast!"

When residents aren't vigilant about keeping bear attractants away, bears are likely to wander from home to home. Often they're just not able to resist the temptation. With such a high reward at stake, bears may override their natural tendency to stay away from people to gain access to the bounty. This can lead to uncharacteristically bold behaviour. Bears tempted with human food are willing to go to great lengths to satisfy their hunger. When then-*Whistler Question* reporter Steven Hill left the kitchen window of his basement suite open "just a crack" one night, a black bear pushed it open further and crawled right in. Hill, who'd moved to Whistler from Montreal the previous month, heard "huffing and snorting" coming from the kitchen. He found the bear sitting on the counter, his head inside a glass cookie jar, every morsel of food from the cupboards and fridge strewn across the floor.

A black bear named Barley was killed by conservation officers in 2007 after breaking into Whistler town Councillor Eckhard Zeidler and his wife Deanne's Bayshores home. Despite the fact that no bear attractants were left out, Barley, who was named after being caught at Whistler's BrewHouse pub and restaurant, was so accustomed to finding food in homes that he entered the Zeidlers' home "on spec." He followed his nose down several flights of stairs to the kitchen.

Preventing Conflicts

To reduce the number of human-bear conflicts, Whistler has a tough wildlife attractant bylaw. It requires residents and visitors to drop off waste and recycling at a "bear-proof" depot. There is no individual public curbside garbage pickup. Hotels, condo complexes and commercial buildings have a private contractor pick up their garbage from bear-proof bins/enclosures. Residents with fruit trees or berry bushes must harvest the fruit regularly and remove fallen fruit from the ground. There are also bear-proof garbage bins along the sidewalk and an electric fence around the waste transfer station. Public composting bins at the recycling depots accept food waste, to discourage backyard composting. Bear-smart behaviour is so ingrained in Whistlerites that one local elementary school has a "no-eating outdoors" policy, to eliminate the possibility of children leaving wrappers or bits of food in the playground.

In Whistler, the policy seems to be working. The number of conflict bears that have been killed has been reduced by more than 50 per cent over the past decade even though the number of human-bear interactions has increased four-fold. Whistler conservation officers say that continued education and enforcement, together with the willingness of most people to comply, has contributed to the improvement.

Whistler is at the forefront of learning to live with its bears, and many communities across North America look to us as a model. Groups like the Get Bear Smart Society, the Whistler Bear Working Group and the Bear Aversion Research Team are helping replace fear and ignorance with understanding and respect.

The Great Contradiction

Like Ursa Major as she shifts position through the sky, society's attitude toward bears has evolved. We no longer believe bears are gods. We don't ascribe supernatural powers to them. Bear bounties and policies of extermination are memories from another era. Today, feeding bears by hand is something only done by tourists who are unaware of both the dangers and the consequences.

Yet there is something about the bear that enraptures us. For many, a chance meeting with a bear is a moment of awe, terror and wonder to be treasured and retold at the coffee shop, on the chairlift, or at the office on Monday morning. People who encounter a bear often say how lucky they were. Some feel fortunate to have been in the presence of such a magnificent animal while others are simply grateful to have survived the encounter.

Bears symbolize the contradiction found in all nature: They are inherently timid, yet potentially dangerous. Gentle, with the capacity to be fierce. Entertaining and playful, yet capable of killing. A bear is your favourite cuddly stuffed animal, morphed into a massive body with sharp teeth and long claws.

Whistlerites are accustomed to contradictions. We work hard and we play hard. We rush to relax. We love our bears, yet we know that giving them what they love—our food—will likely result in their death. If we don't spoil them with human contact and human food, bears can live peacefully in the surrounding area with quiet dignity. They wander the same forests we do, den on our ski hill, and devour the flowers we photograph. And although they have the power to cause serious harm, they choose not to.

The bears of Whistler remind us that we live in a small pocket of a vast wilderness. It is a complicated land, full of mystery, tragedy, beauty and joy. In sharing this land with one of the world's most fascinating creations, we create a narrative that is unique and complex. It's a story that is perhaps best told in pictures. It's a Whistler Bear Story.

jeanie

A Local Icon

It's January, and deep inside a hollow in an old growth tree under Blackcomb Mountain's Peak 2 Peak gondola, three black bears are born. Snow banks around the den protect the tiny cubs from the frigid air and biting wind as they nuzzle into their mom's fur and suckle her fat-rich milk. This is Jeanie's sixth litter.

At about 20 years old, Jeanie is probably Whistler's best-known bear. She has a distinctive swath of white fur across her chest, mottled with darker blotches. Some say the markings on her face make her look as if she's wearing old-fashioned spectacles.

By spring, Jeanie and her new family emerge from their den. The cubs, no bigger than house cats, are skittish. Even the wind rustling the branches can send the three scampering up a tree. They play with whatever they can find—sticks, rocks, pinecones, and of course, mom. They climb all over her, bouncing off her head, jumping on her back, rolling under her legs. She occasionally grunts, telling them to stay close. Her patience seems infinite.

While they are small, Jeanie must protect her cubs from the constant threat of coyotes and cougars, as well as from adult male bears that sometimes kill cubs so they can mate with the mother and produce their own litters. She also has to watch out for her rival Katie, who is slowly gaining ground in the bruin hierarchy and has been challenging the aging Jeanie for dominance.

Jeanie and her cubs' summer range encompasses the vast coastal hemlock and cedar forests on the north slope of Whistler Mountain and the south slope of Blackcomb. It's an area that has seen increased development and recreational activities over the past decade. The bears now share their territory with ATVs, Hummers, construction workers and their heavy equipment, the Whistler Bike Park, and thousands of hikers and bear-watchers. Jeanie has adapted well to the activity, and is tolerant of humans.

However, fewer berries and increased competition for natural food has meant Jeanie has taken her cubs on some dangerous outings into Whistler Village. Each time she ventures into town and is rewarded with human food or garbage, her behaviour is reinforced, increasing the risk of coming into conflict and getting killed for being a human safety risk. One of her most serious infractions occurred when she climbed over the counter of Zogs, a popular outdoor fast-food restaurant in the Village, and ate her fill of hotdogs and buns.

PHOTO BY IRENE SHEPPARD

Whenever she's in town, researchers and conservation officers use non-lethal aversion techniques to scare her away. The goal is to teach Jeanie that populated areas equal pain and discomfort. She has been yelled at, shot with rubber bullets, chased by a trained Karelian bear dog and pelted with marbles from a sling shot.

It was not her interaction with humans that caused the death of Jeanie's most recent litter. One by one the cubs disappeared; researchers suspect natural predators or adult male bears—or perhaps even Katie—killed them. Unfortunately, the loss of her offspring is not new to Jeanie. Most of the 12 cubs she has had since 1997 have eventually died in vehicle accidents, attacks by natural predators, or by being shot or relocated by officials.

A bear's existence can be brutal, but Jeanie carries on, accepting both life's tragedies and its gifts. In early September of 2009, two different males, including a large boar named Slumber, were seen courting Jeanie. And so the cycle continues.

^

Bear cubs are born during winter denning, usually in mid-January. At first they are about the size of a squirrel, cannot see, and are covered with fine, downy hair. Once they have left the womb, they find their way to their mother's teats where they nurse, sleep and grow until spring. Hibernating female bears are the only mammal to lactate for up to three months without eating. She can produce a litter of up to five or six cubs every two years. In Whistler the average is two cubs per litter. When they emerge from the den, healthy bear cubs weigh about five to eight pounds.

▲
Who knows what made Alice's five-month-old cubs scamper up a tree. They could have been trying to escape a predator, they could have been scared by human activity, or maybe they were just being playful. Whatever the reason, a treetop is a fairly safe place for cubs to hang out, and mom can continue to forage without worrying about her babies. A large predator like a cougar or even another bear would never be able to climb to the small upper branches that can only support the cubs' weight.

▸▸
It's all fun and games now, but what these cubs learn by playing and wrestling could help them survive serious encounters later in life. Play is most elaborate and prolonged in young mammals whose behaviour as adults is based in large part on learning—animals like bears, dogs, cats, and primates. However, few animals play more than bear cubs do. It seems these cubs just wanna have fun.

Elly enjoys the company and playful antics of her three cubs. Although mother bears are affectionate, protective, devoted, and sensitive guardians until the cubs are old enough to survive on their own, only about half of all bear cubs live to see their first birthday. Infanticide is not uncommon in the bear world. Male bears sometimes prey on the wee, helpless critters to bring the female back into estrus, allowing the male to mate with her and propagate his own genes.

Depending on food abundance, a mother may keep her cubs with her after their first birthday, denning together again and breaking up the family in the third year. Elly was one of those mothers.

Bears love dandelions and other greens in spring when their stems are tender. As summer progresses, cellulose forms around the cell walls of many plants and weeds, making them difficult for bears to digest.

fitz

Looking for Love and Cookies

Fitz was the Big Daddy-O of Whistler bears. At 300 pounds, this laid-back black love bruin seemed to be both a deep thinker and a playboy. He could often be seen chilling out on Blackcomb Mountain in a Buddha-style seated position, as if contemplating the great philosophical conundrums of life, two gigantic paws laid gently upon his knees, the tag on his ear looking like the piercing of a rebel. Most days, a sweet young female bear wouldn't be far off, biding her time while he finished "meditating" so they could mate. Fitz seems to have paired up with pretty much all the female bears on Blackcomb and Whistler mountains. A grunt and a huff were his best pick-up lines; they worked every time.

He tolerated photographers and bear-viewers, but was not enamoured with people, often giving them the "leave me alone" stare before going about his business. Old Fitz saved his true passion for his furry female friends.

For most of his life, Fitz stayed away from town, living peacefully off berries and grubs in the mountains. Unfortunately, after one particularly bad berry season Fitz wandered further than usual to fill his belly, and discovered the allure of garbage. Smelly food scraps provided a "gateway drug;" an easy way for him to gain the calories his huge body required without nearly as much effort as picking berries. It wasn't long before Fitz was breaking into garages and sheds for his next fix.

In 2007, Fitz discovered that even more food was up for grabs if he went straight to the source: the kitchen. Through screen doors and open windows he'd make his way into homes to fill up on cookies, muffins, fruit, and whatever else was available. Fridges, cupboards and countertops were his buffet, and the patriarch of the bear community was hooked.

Fitz was shot in 2008 after breaking into a house in Whistler Cay Heights for a loaf of bread. A woman alone with her small child in the house screamed at him, scaring him away. Her friend called Whistler Bear Response Officers, who were on the scene when he boldly returned to attempt to finish the meal he'd started.

Fitz was twenty years old.

Emerald is a demure and tolerant female who was first live-trapped by researchers at the base of Whistler's Emerald chairlift. She takes advantage of the abundant clover planted to re-vegetate the green space in the middle of the Sliding Centre—an Olympic venue for the 2010 Vancouver/Whistler Games. Clover is a favourite spring food for bears; it is highly nutritious when it first emerges.

«

Alpine is a gigantic brute of a bear who has been involved in many scraps with other bears, earning him the nicknames Scarface and The Belly Dragger. Tipping the scale at 484 pounds when he was live-trapped by conservation officers in the fall of 2008, Alpine is the largest bear ever caught in the area.

˅

Bears are highly evolved social animals with intelligence comparable to that of great apes. They often share friendship, resources and security. But sometimes, like humans, bears like to simply sit alone, stretch out their legs and enjoy the day.

Courtship, which marks the start of mating season, begins mid-May. This is normally the only time adult males and females entertain each other's company. It can last from several days to a few weeks. To kick things off, a male suitor trails his prospective mate from a distance, smelling her daybeds and sniffing her urine to analyze how receptive she is to mating. At first, she may run away, playing hard to get. In time, she allows him closer and closer. If she is afraid, she may even charge him or swat him with her paw. Males rarely retaliate, but bide their time. When contact is made, the bears nuzzle and chew on each other's head and neck and may even engage in some playful wrestling before they are ready to breed.

The average age for female black bears to first breed is 3½ years old. At 20 years old, Jeanie proves that bears remain fertile well into their senior years. Males also reach sexual maturity at roughly 3½ years old, but they rarely have the opportunity to prove their virility when they are young because of intense competition from older, bigger males, who tend to be the most prolific breeders.

▲

Although the female is in heat for several weeks, usually between May and July, she will only allow a male to mount her when she is most receptive, in the three to five day period in the middle of her estrus cycle. During those mating days, the male and female become virtually inseparable, mating repeatedly, eating and sleeping together. Copulation itself normally lasts 20 to 30 minutes, but may continue for up to one hour, with the couple sometimes breaking to nuzzle each other, have a play fight, or take a quick walk before resuming.

However, bears of both sexes are far from monogamous. Cubs from the same litter may even have different fathers. Implantation of the fertilized egg(s) in the female's womb is delayed until the start of denning season. The number of cubs born is determined by the amount of weight the mother gains. If she gains sufficient body fat during the summer and fall, the embryos will attach to the uterine wall and develop into little bears. Otherwise, they will dissolve. It's Mother Nature's way of keeping the bear population in check.

katie

The Wild Card

Katie is a black bear who is easy to identify but difficult to understand. Her thick, dark coat is punctuated by a solid white V-shape on her chest. She challenges commonly held assumptions about bear behaviour, perplexing researchers and sending observers away scratching their heads.

As a general rule, female bears don't attack another mother's cubs. But Katie did. Although she didn't kill them, she attacked Jeanie's two 5½-month-old cubs. Twice.

Female bears don't usually stay with their own cubs for more than a year. But Katie did. She kept her two black cubs, mirror images of herself, at her side for 2½ years.

Female bears don't often den near human activity. But Katie did. She denned approximately 10 meters off Whistler's ski-out one winter, even producing a healthy litter of cubs there.

Katie is smaller than most of the other mountain matriarchs, but what she lacks in girth, she makes up for in attitude. She does not like to be near people, retreats quickly when she encounters anyone, and never comes into town. Once, when she was trapped to be radio-collared for research, Katie pulled her lips back, gathered bile from deep within her throat, and spat heartily on an observer. It was the only time in a dozen years of observing and photographing bears that Sylvia Dolson had ever been spat on. The tarry, black substance covered her from head to toe, and could in no way be construed as a sign of affection.

Katie's unique personality and uncommon behaviour has made her a favorite among bear-watchers and researchers, if for nothing else but to see what she'll do next. Like the wild card on a reality TV show, she can appear cold and aloof, yet we can't help being fascinated by her. There is something irresistible about Katie's eccentric nature.

▲
While the majority of her day is spent foraging for food, this mother finds a few moments to rest her paws as her cubs nap above in a coastal hemlock tree.

▸▸
This young female is still trying to establish her own home range on Whistler Mountain. While mothers allow their daughters to stay in their natal ranges, young males are forced out. These dispersing males are often forced into urban areas by more dominant males who claim the best habitat for themselves.

⮝⮜

Bears enjoy cottonwood catkins, elderberry, skunk cabbage, salmon berries, blueberries, huckleberries and high bush cranberries. With no access to salmon in Whistler, bears add protein to their diet with ants, grubs and caterpillars. They also eat greens such as clover, grasses, sedges and horsetail.

⮞⮞

This young male displays a defensive posture with his nose drawn down and lips squared off. He's huffing (expelling air loudly) and clacking his teeth to warn intruders to back off. Understanding a black bear's body language and heeding his warnings help keep encounters safe and conflict-free.

▲
Bears live in a rich and complex scent-defined world, where messages are transferred, information is gathered and warnings are given through smell alone. Airborne scent, scent transferred to twigs, branches and grass, scent left on purpose by tree rubbing, as well as scat or urine marks, combine to form the ursine version of a daily newspaper. With 100 times more nasal mucosa area than in the human nose, bears are able to understand far more about the world through their sense of smell than we can.

Bears also have better hearing than we do. Like dogs, they can hear pitches that exceed human frequency range and sensitivity. And contrary to popular belief, bears have fairly good eyesight, especially close-up. They have full-colour vision, are able to see well day and night, and have an extraordinary ability to distinguish moving objects.

^
Scratches and bite marks on trees, bits of fur stuck on the bark and tracks on the ground are all signs that there are bears in the area.

Bear tracks are easy to distinguish from canine or feline tracks because bears have five toes. In fact, bears' rear tracks look surprisingly similar to human footsteps.

The hollow tree opening (top right) has some bits of fur stuck to the bark, indicating that a bear has likely used this space for his winter home.

>
Bears are strong and powerful animals. They have been known to pry open car doors and windows in search of food. Bears routinely roll over huge rocks and logs looking for insects. This rotting log was torn apart by a bear looking for grubs and ants inside.

>
Scat is the most obvious sign that bears are in the area. The characteristics of black bear scat depend on the size of the bear and his diet. It's easy to guess what the bears responsible for the scat in the photos had been eating—berries, grass and birdseed.

marissa

One Tough Mama

Marissa used to be known as the bear that limped.

Exactly how she hurt herself is a mystery, but for several months she dragged her lame front right leg beneath her without putting any weight on it.

Injuries are not uncommon among bears—hers could have occurred during a tussle with another bear, she could have fallen from a tree or simply tripped while walking along a rocky slope.

But life for a black bear in the mountains is all about survival, and an injury won't stop her from doing what she needs to do: eat. Late summer and fall is berry season, a time when the huckleberries and mountain ash berries growing above mid-mountain are at their best, and bears must bulk up for the winter. Lame leg or not, it's gorge-time.

So on a crisp autumn day, Marissa carefully positions herself in the midst of a bush dripping with succulent fruits. Her black lips flop, her tongue slurps and she rhythmically gulps down as many as she can. She's hungry, but she's conscientious, and plucks only the sweetest, juiciest berries. If they aren't ripe, she leaves them behind, and returns to check on the "crop" later in the week. With eyes searching the bush for more blue and purple treats, she's always anticipating her next mouthful. Marissa swallows the berries whole; chewing is a waste of time for a bear. She virtually vacuums the bush before moving methodically to the next meal-station.

Not only is she an excellent fruit harvester, Marissa is also a highly efficient farmer. Thousands of undigested berry seeds in her scat are spread throughout her territory,

some taking root and creating new plants for upcoming generations. Her scat also provides welcome food for birds and small ungulates, who can't resist the undigested berry skins and seeds in the piles.

Marissa no longer limps. Researchers now identify this 20-year-old matriarch by her distinctly feminine facial features, light brown muzzle and the small white blaze on her chest. While she and her cubs have been known to feed on the greens at the Chateau Whistler golf course, Marissa generally stays away from people.

She is a regal, aloof, shy, beautiful bear, with a tough streak humans can never quite know the depth of.

▲
It's late October and the early snowfall is a sure sign of winter's impending arrival. This curious 2½-year-old stands up to get a better look at whatever sparked his interest. It's much easier for him to see, smell and hear from an upright position than from down on all fours.

►►
The open meadows of Whistler's ski areas are excellent grazing areas for black bears, and it's easy to bear-watch from gondolas and chairlifts. Bear-viewing tours are also offered by Whistler-Blackcomb several times daily during bear season.

➤
Fitz grazes on horsetail among the lupins; a perfect photo opportunity. Dusk and dawn are the best times to view and photograph bears, when milder temperatures and reduced human activity make foraging more comfortable. If you are taking pictures, stay at least 100 meters away from the bear and use a telephoto lens.

The best bear-watching starts mid-May, when bears and possibly wee cubs emerge from their dens and seek spring greenery on ski runs and golf courses. Because there is still snow at higher elevations in the spring, bears are concentrated close to the valley floor. By July, when snow melts and berries begin to ripen, bears are more difficult to spot. They disperse to higher elevations around the mountains and spend much of their time in the thick of berry bushes, some of which tower over them. By October, the berry crop is depleted and bears retreat to the valley bottom once again. At this time, they graze on golf course greens, munch fall berries on mountain ash trees and may even go after human garbage.

slip

Before You Bin It,
Think What's In It!
Is it recyclable???
If it is, it doesn't go
in the GARBAGE!!!
For the safety
of you and
the
BEARS
PLEASE CLOSE
compactor doors
OPEN
GARBAGE COMPACTOR

A Loveable Oaf

Slip was one of those bears you couldn't help but root for. He meant no harm, but like any teenage boy, he seemed to find trouble wherever he went, leaving his grimy paw prints behind as evidence. Originally named Max when he was born on Blackcomb Mountain in 2003, Slip, a bear being studied by researchers, acquired his nickname after slipping out of his radio collar three times.

PHOTO BY NICOLA BRABYN

Slip tagged along with his mother Marissa for about a year before expanding his home range. This is natural behaviour for a young male bear, but Slip soon found himself in some unnatural places and learned some very unnatural things. When he was in town, he figured out how to access pedestrian waste bins. When his paws were still small, he managed to squeeze them into the supposedly bear-proof latch and open the lid. Soon, his paws grew too big to fit into the handle, but Slip didn't give up. He'd test every bin he passed to see if it looked tippable or if the back door was locked—an easy score if it wasn't.

PHOTOS BY IRENE SHEPPARD

Slip was a social fellow. He was a member of what researchers called The Fitz Creek Gang, a group of five unrelated male and female bears, all around the same age, who would hang out on the ski hill, playing with and pulling down snow fencing and signs. They also enjoyed a good frolic in the snow. It wasn't unusual to see several gang members wrestling and sliding together down a patch of snow at Blackcomb Base II in the spring. Although they never ventured into town as a group, the Fitz Creek bears were all seen individually prowling for human food in the Village.

Slip was a clever bear, an expert at getting what he wanted. One hot summer day when he needed to cool off, he made his way into a hotel pool for a refreshing dip. And once he walked into the loading bay at the Westin Hotel, climbed some stairs, walked about 50 meters down a hallway and entered the hotel garbage compactor looking for food.

Conservation officers, bylaw officers and RCMP repeatedly applied non-lethal aversive conditioning techniques. Slip was hazed 39 times in the fall of 2005 to deter him from venturing into populated areas. The following year, the Bear Aversion Research Team (BART) conducted an even more intensive aversive conditioning program on him. For over a week, Slip was monitored day and night, hit with rubber bullets and moved out whenever he tried to access the Village. He was persistent in his attempts to get what he wanted, but he never harmed a soul.

By the time the snow melted in 2007, there was speculation that Slip may have turned over a new leaf. He hadn't been in trouble in town since reappearing from his den. However, spring is when bears look for mates, and that's likely what he was preoccupied with.

Slip never got the chance to prove whether he'd been "reformed." The loveable trouble-maker was shot by a hunter in the Soo Valley in May, 2007, when he was just four years old.

⌃
Two members of the Fitz Creek Gang wrestle in the backyards of the Montebello townhomes before slipping into the wetlands adjacent to Lost Lake Park.

➤⌃
DaVinci got his name when he was caught by the Bear Aversion Research Team (BART) at the Paintball Field. He is a frequent visitor to Nicklaus North Golf Course outside berry season.

➤
Grass is not a bear's first choice for a meal. But during early spring and late fall, other more nutritious foods may not be available, and grass on golf courses offer enough calories to sustain their weight. Whistler golfers are accustomed to sharing golf course greens with local bruins, who, in return, enhance the experience for golfers with their presence.

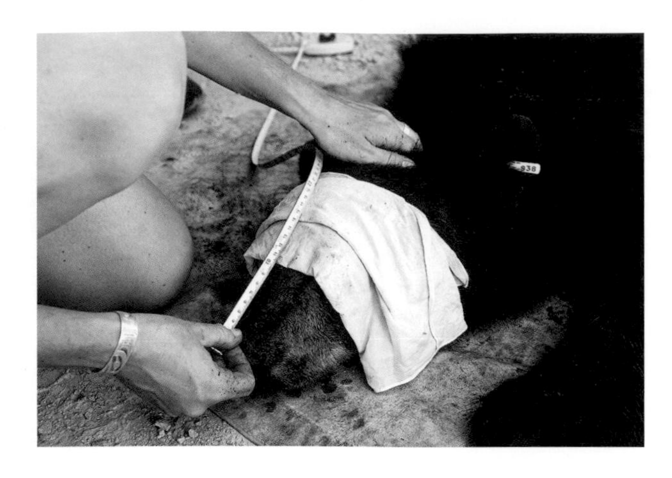

^

Biologists measure the skull, paw, neck, heart, body length and abdominal girth of each bear they study. This gives scientists a good idea of the bear's health and how he compares in size to other bears in the area.

v

A biologist checks that Katie's radio collar is not too tight. The collar is not intended to be permanent. A piece of cotton fire hose inserted between the two ends of the collar will eventually rot and the collar will fall off, ensuring she isn't collared for the rest of her life.

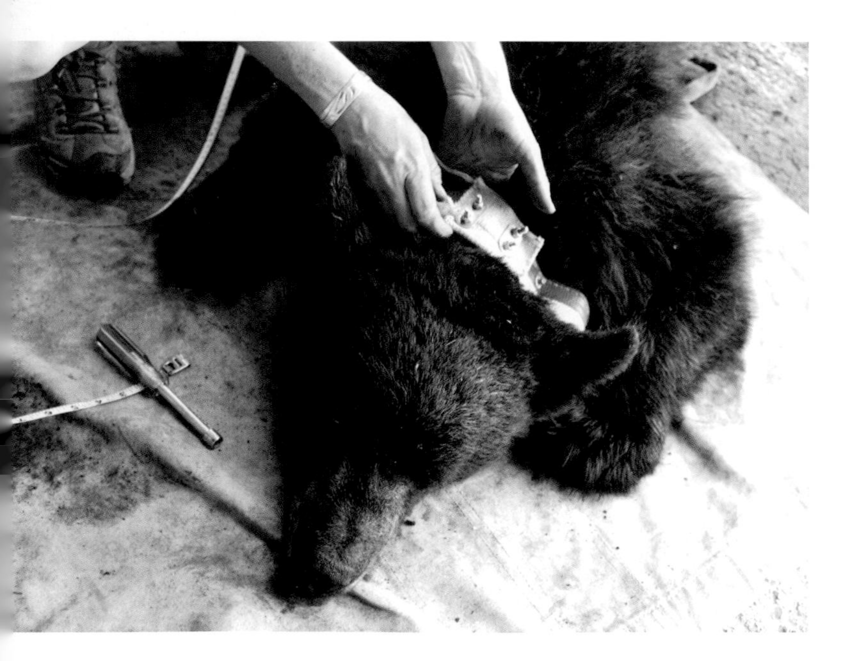

^

Slip is immobilized by a conservation officer. The young bear will be fitted with a radio collar so researchers can monitor his movements and learn about his daily life.

>>

So-called "problem" bears are not born; they are the product of human carelessness and indifference. Although not all bears end up in conflict with people, those that frequent developed areas where garbage and other bear attractants are easily accessible are much more likely to get into trouble.

v

Researchers collect a blood sample from Katie. When she recovers from the effects of the drugs, she will be released on Whistler Mountain where she was captured.

<
Like people, bears have a wide range of emotions and personalities. Bears can be fearful, joyful, playful and social. These two bears are enjoying each other's company as they enter the courtship phase before mating.

▼
Bears often forage close to roadways in early spring to take advantage of the emerging grasses and clover. Newly-seeded areas are favourite feeding grounds. This puts bears and people at risk. Collisions are often fatal for bears and cause significant damage to vehicles.

PHOTO BY IRENE SHEPPARD

About the Author/Photographer

Sylvia Dolson's passion for bears is equaled only by her quest to teach people about the true nature of these wonderful bruins. Her ultimate goal is for a greater coexistence—one in which people and bears live in harmony. As a naturalist, wildlife photographer and freelance writer, Sylvia chooses to spend much of her free time in the company of bears. Having walked among wild black bears, polar bears and grizzlies, she has gained an ever-increasing appreciation and understanding of all the wilderness and its inhabitants.

Sylvia has been involved with the Get Bear Smart Society since 1996 and is now the executive director. She is also a member of the International Association for Bear Research and Management. As a leading expert on living with bears in residential communities, she has been instrumental in bringing forward more progressive, bear-friendly management policies in British Columbia, Canada. She currently co-chairs the Whistler Bear Working Group and was the key catalyst and contributor for Whistler's Black Bear Management Plan. Her persistent hard work and dedication have resulted in establishing Whistler as British Columbia's leading Bear Smart community, becoming a model for others to follow.

Sylvia travels throughout North America speaking at conferences and workshops. She has authored many reference materials for educational purposes, maintains an extensive website, and writes a regular newspaper column. She is also the author of *Bear~ology: Fascinating Bear Facts, Tales & Trivia.*

Sylvia and her husband, Steve, live in Whistler, British Columbia, where they share their lives with two canine companions, Samantha and Brandy.

To reach Sylvia Dolson, please email info@bearsmart.com.

About the Writer

Katherine Fawcett is an award-winning freelance and creative writer. She has lived, hiked, run and skied in bear country for almost 20 years both in Canmore, AB, and the Whistler/Pemberton, BC, area. Yet every time she sees a bear, it still takes her breath away.

Katherine is the author of the children's book *Mushkid: A Tale of Dogsledding, Friendship and Drool*. She has contributed to magazines and newspapers across Canada and has a weekly poetry column in *The Pembertonian News*. Her literary awards include: first place in EVENT Magazine's creative non-fiction contest, 2009; first place in the Federation of BC Writers short fiction competition, 2008; and first place in the Vicious Circle's Whistler Untold creative non-fiction contest, 2008. She was a finalist in the Writers' Union of Canada's Writing for Children contest in 2009, and a category winner in CBC Radio's six-word story contest in 2008. She is currently working on a collection of short stories.

For more information, visit www.katherinefawcett.com.

PHOTO BY ANASTASIA CHOMLACK

About the Get Bear Smart Society

The Get Bear Smart Society (GBS), based in Whistler, British Columbia, Canada, champions progressive management policies that reduce both the number of human-bear conflicts and the number of bears destroyed. Our mission is to provide a safe environment in which people and bears can coexist in harmony. We accomplish this by implementing effective waste management systems, educating people on dealing with bears in their communities as well as minimizing backyard attractants, and promoting innovative, non-lethal bear management practices.

Bearsmart.com is the most popular resource for information on living with bears, recreating in bear country, and learning about bear biology and ecology. The site also contains information for policy makers and bear aware groups on creating bear-smart communities and offers innovative, non-lethal bear management techniques for bear managers.

Please consider making a donation to help support bear-smart initiatives. Don't forget to visit our online store at www.bearsmart.com/store to check out our playing cards, books and other fun and educational products.

Get Bear Smart Society
P.O. Box 502
Whistler, BC V0N 1B0 Canada

www.bearsmart.com
Email: info@bearsmart.com